The British Subjugation of Australia: The History of British Colonization and the Conquest of the Aboriginal Australians

By Charles River Editors

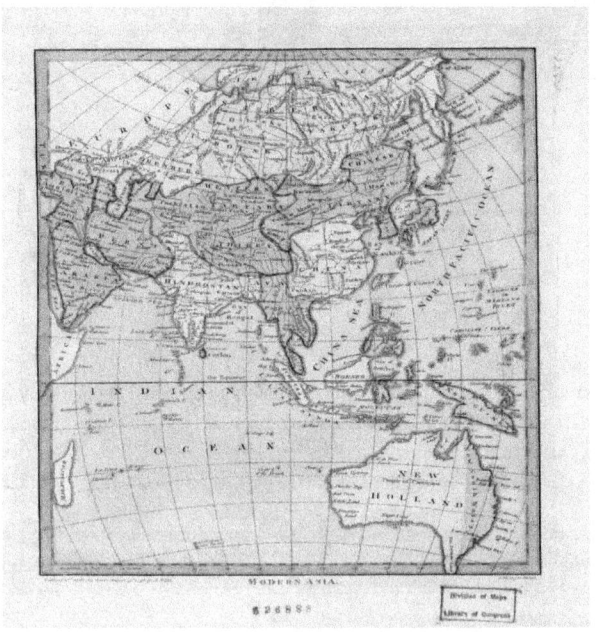

A 1796 map depicting the region

About Charles River Editors

Charles River Editors is a boutique digital publishing company, specializing in bringing history back to life with educational and engaging books on a wide range of topics. Keep up to date with our new and free offerings with this 5 second sign up on our weekly mailing list, and visit Our Kindle Author Page to see other recently published Kindle titles.

We make these books for you and always want to know our readers' opinions, so we encourage you to leave reviews and look forward to publishing new and exciting titles each week.

Introduction

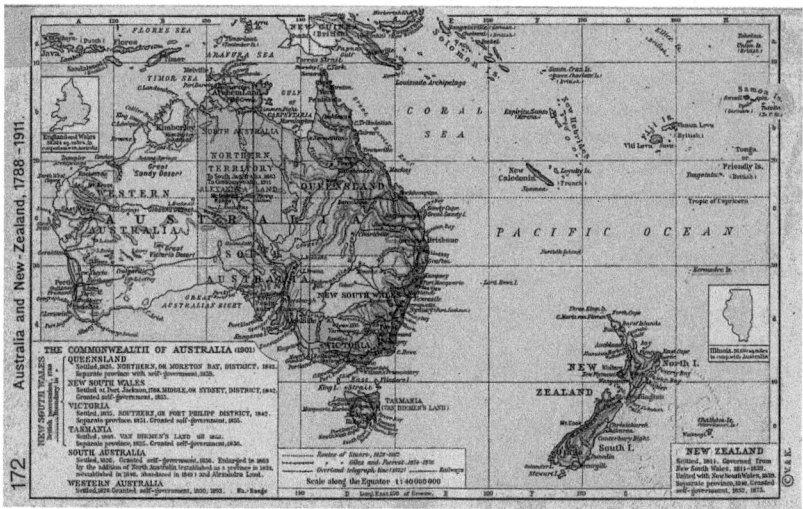

The Subjugation of Australia

"It is quite time that our children were taught a little more about their country, for shame's sake." – Henry Lawson, Australian poet

A land of almost 3 million square miles has lain since time immemorial on the southern flank of the planet, so isolated that it remained almost entirely outside of European knowledge until 1770. From there, however, the subjugation of Australia would take place rapidly. Within 20 years of the first British settlements being established, the British presence in Terra Australis was secure, and no other major power was likely to mount a challenge. In 1815, Napoleon would be defeated at Waterloo, and soon afterwards would be standing on the barren cliffs of Saint Helena, staring across the limitless Atlantic. The French, without a fleet, were out of the picture, the Germans were yet to establish a unified state, let alone an overseas empire of any significance, and the Dutch were no longer counted among the top tier of European powers.

Australia lay at an enormous distance from London, and its administration was barely supervised. Thus, its development was slow in the beginning, and its function remained narrowly defined, but as the 19th century progressed and peace took hold over Europe, things began to change. Immigration was steady, and the small spores of European habitation on the continent steadily grew. At the same time, the Royal Navy found itself with enormous resources of men and ships at a time when there was no war to fight. British sailors were thus employed for survey and exploration work, and the great expanses of Australia attracted particular interest. It was an exciting time, and an exciting age - the world was slowly coming under European sway, and Britain was rapidly emerging as its leader.

That said, the 19th century certainly wasn't exciting for the people who already lived in Australia. The history of the indigenous inhabitants of Australia, known in contemporary anthropology as the "Aboriginal and Torres Strait Islander people of Australia," is a complex and continually evolving field of study, and it has been colored by politics. For generations after the arrival of whites in Australia, the Aboriginal people were disregarded and marginalized, largely because they offered little in the way of a labor resource, and they occupied land required for European settlement.

At the same time, it is a misconception that indigenous Australians meekly accepted the invasion of their country by the British, for they did not. They certainly resisted, but as far as colonial wars during that era went, the frontier conflicts of Australia did not warrant a great deal of attention. Indigenous Australians were hardly a warlike people, and without central organization, or political cohesion beyond scattered family groups, they succumbed to the orchestrated advance of white settlement with passionate, but futile resistance. In many instances, aggressive clashes between the two groups simply gave the white colonists reasonable cause to inflict a style of genocide on the Aborigines that stood in the way of progress.

In any case, their fate had largely been sealed by the first European sneeze in the Terra Australis, which preceded the importation of the two signature mediums of social destruction. The first was a collection of alien diseases, chief among smallpox, but also cholera, influenza, measles, tuberculosis, syphilis and the common cold. The second was alcohol. Smallpox alone killed more than 50% of the aboriginal population, and once the fabric of indigenous society had crumbled, alcohol provided emotional relief, but relegated huge numbers of Aborigines to the margins of a robust and emerging colonial society.

The British Subjugation of Australia: The History of British Colonization and the Conquest of the Aboriginal Australians analyzes the rapid colonization and the ramifications for everyone on the continent. Along with pictures of important people, places, and events, you will learn about the subjugation of Australia like never before.

The British Subjugation of Australia: The History of British Colonization and the Conquest of the Aboriginal Australians
About Charles River Editors
Introduction
   The British Claim
   Development and Expansion
   Further Exploration
   The End of the Dream
   The Founding of Western Australia
   South Australia and Tasmania
   The End of the Convict Era
   Online Resources
   Bibliography
Free Books by Charles River Editors
Discounted Books by Charles River Editors

The British Claim

The earliest entry by Europeans upon the Indian Ocean was by the Portuguese mariner Bartholomew Dias, who rounded the Cape of Storms (later the Cape of Good Hope) in 1488. He ventured no further than the confluence of the Atlantic and Indian Oceans, and it would not be for another decade that his compatriot Vasco da Gama pressed his discoveries further east to the coast of India. The Portuguese then established a presence on the east coast of Africa, and with the entire Orient to themselves, undertook numerous voyages of exploration, not all of which were directly recorded. There is, therefore, a school of thought advocating the notion that it was the Portuguese who were the first Europeans to lay eyes on the great southern land. Supporting this theory are ancient Portuguese maps of a coast that may well be Australia, and occasional relics of Portuguese origin that have been found in various places in Australia.

Perhaps the most compelling argument in favor of prior Portuguese discovery is logic. The Portuguese established colonies in India and various other points in Southeast Asia, with Portuguese Timor a mere 400 miles from the Australian coast. Bearing in mind the scope of Portuguese maritime exploration, there is no reason at all to assume that the Portuguese would not have followed the natural progression of the Malay Archipelago to arrive precisely on the north shore of Terra Australis. This would certainly be in character, and as early Portuguese mariners cruised the Malay Archipelago, it seems almost inevitable that they would have bumped into Australia. They could hardly have conceived of what it was, but it would nonetheless have given them prior claim.

Nonetheless, in the end, it was Dutch mariner Willem Janszoon, aboard the Dutch East India Company vessel Duyfken, who claimed those laurels. It is now an accepted fact that his expedition was the first to touch the shores of what would today be the northern tip of Queensland.

Janszoon was followed very soon afterwards by a Spanish expedition led by Portuguese navigator Pedro Fernandes de Queirós. This small fleet arrived from the east, having made numerous smaller discoveries en route around Cape Horn. Queirós in fact mistakenly took the New Hebrides to be the much-storied southern continent, so he named it Austrialia del Espiritu Santo, or the Southern Land of the Holy Spirit, in honor of the Spanish queen Margaret of Austria. The next to broach the horizon was a subordinate captain of Queirós named Luís Vaz de Torres, who sailed in from the east in July 1606. Sticking to the south shore of Papua, New Guinea, he passed through Torres Strait, which was subsequently named after him. He paused briefly on the northern tip of Cape York before continuing on through the Malay Archipelago.

For the remainder of the 17th century, frequent Dutch visits would be made to the coast of this vast and enigmatic land, and thanks to this it was nominally claimed by the Dutch, who called it New Holland. They were not disposed to settle and colonize, however; the Dutch were primarily a mercantile people, and their objectives were gold, spices, slaves, and occasional Christian missionary work. The coast of Australia appeared to have nothing of direct interest to these Dutch mariners, which ensured they moved on.

Thus, by the 1700s, the existence of the Terra Australis was generally known and understood, and incrementally, its shores were observed and mapped. With that said, the southern coast would not be mapped in detail until the 19th century, but Van Diemen's Land, an island off the south coast now called Tasmania, was identified in 1642 by Dutch mariner Abel Tasman. A few months later, this intrepid Dutchman would add New Zealand to the map of the known world.

The English were the greatest naval power in Europe, but they arrived on the scene rather later. The first to appear was William Dampier, captain of the HMS *Roebuck*, in 1699, after he had been granted a Royal Commission by King William III to explore the east coast of New Holland. By then, the general global balance of power was shifting, and with the English gaining a solid foothold in India, their supremacy in the Indian Ocean trade zone began. The Dutch, once predominant in the region, began slowly to lose ground, slipping out of contention as a major global trading power. So too were the Portuguese, also once dominant in the region. It was now just the French and the English who were facing one another down in a quest to dominate the world, but their imperial interests were focused mainly in India and the East Indies, as well as the Caribbean and the Americas. As a result, the potential of a vast, practically uninhabited great southern continent did not hold much interest.

Between the 1699 expedition of William Dampier and the 1770 expedition of the HMS *Endeavour*, little European traffic disturbed the epochal slumber of Australia. However, times were changing. As the *Endeavor* weighed anchor and slipped out of Botany Bay, Marie-Antoinette was betrothed to King Louis XVI of France, and the French Revolution was on the horizon. In the United Kingdom itself, the Catholic King James II of England had been overthrown by a coalition of Parliamentarians and the Protestant William of Orange, which triggered an economic and capital revival in England, the founding of the Bank of England, and a massive extension of the interests and influence of the mighty British East India Company.

By then the world was largely mapped, with just regions such as the Arctic Archipelago and the two poles remaining terra incognita. A few gaps needed to be filled in here and there, but all of the essential details were known. At the same time, a great deal of imperial energy was at play in Europe, particularly in Britain. Britain stood at the cusp of global dominance thanks almost entirely to the Royal Navy, which emerged in the 17th and 18th centuries as an institution significantly more than the sum of its parts. With vast assets available even in peacetime, expeditions of science and explorations were launched in every direction. This was done not only to claim ownership of the field of global exploration, but also to undercut the imperial ambitions of others, in particular the French.

In 1767, the Royal Society persuaded King George III to allocate funds for it to send an astronomer to the Pacific, and on January 1, 1768, the London Annual Register reported, "Mr.

Banks, Dr. Solander, and Mr. Green the astronomer, set out for Deal, to embark on board the Endeavour, Captain Cook, for the South Seas, under the direction of the royal society, to observe the transit of Venus next summer, and to make discoveries." Mr. Banks was Joseph Banks, a botanist, and he brought along Dr. Daniel Solander, a Swedish naturalist. Charles Green was at that time the assistant to Nevil Maskelyne, the Astronomer Royal. The expedition, which would leave later in 1768, would be captained by Cook, a war veteran who had recently fought in the French & Indian War against the French in North America.

King George III

Banks

Solander

What the article did not mention was that the Admiralty was also hoping to find the famed Terra Australis Incognita, the legendary "unknown southern land." This came out later, when the *London Gazetteer* reported on August 18, 1768, "The gentlemen, who are to sail in a few days for George's Land, the new discovered island in the Pacific ocean, with an intention to observe the Transit of Venus, are likewise, we are credibly informed, to attempt some new discoveries in that vast unknown tract, above the latitude 40." As this suggests, the British already knew that there was a mostly unexplored landmass in the region, and this is because Europeans had sighted the coast of Australia over 150 years earlier.

When Captain James Cook's expedition began in 1768, it included more than 80 men, consisting of 73 sailors and 12 members of the Royal Marines. Presumably, the expedition was supposed to be for entirely scientific – and hence peaceful – purposes. The *Endeavour* left Plymouth on August 26, 1768, and Cook landed at Matavai Bay, Tahiti, on April 13, 1769. The most important task at hand, other than day-to-day survival, was preparing to observe the transit of Venus that would occur on June 3.

Having completed the scientific assignments, the *Endeavour* next set sail in search of Terra Australis. After sailing for nearly two months, the crew earned the prize of being only the second group of Europeans to ever visit New Zealand. They arrived on October 6, 1769, and Cook described a harrowing experience when the men came ashore: "MONDAY, 9th October. …I went ashore with a Party of men in the Pinnace and yawl accompanied by Mr. Banks and Dr. Solander. We landed abreast of the Ship and on the East side of the River just mentioned; but seeing some of the Natives on the other side of the River of whom I was desirous of speaking with, and finding that we could not ford the River, I order'd the yawl in to carry us over, and the pinnace to lay at the Entrance. In the mean time the Indians made off. However we went as far as their Hutts which lay about 2 or 300 Yards from the water side, leaving 4 boys to take care of the Yawl, which we had no sooner left than 4 Men came out of the woods on the other side the River, and would certainly have cut her off had not the People in the Pinnace discover'd them and called to her to drop down the Stream, which they did, being closely persued by the Indians. The coxswain of the Pinnace, who had the charge of the Boats, seeing this, fir'd 2 Musquets over their Heads; the first made them stop and Look round them, but the 2nd they took no notice of; upon which a third was fir'd and kill'd one of them upon the Spot just as he was going to dart his spear at the Boat. At this the other 3 stood motionless for a Minute or two, seemingly quite surprised; wondering, no doubt, what it was that had thus kill'd their Comrade; but as soon as they recovered themselves they made off, dragging the Dead body a little way and then left it. Upon our hearing the report of the Musquets we immediately repair'd to the Boats, and after viewing the Dead body we return'd on board."

Over the following weeks, Cook devoted himself to making a detailed map of the New Zealand coast. Sailing west, Cook hoped to reach Van Diemen's Land, known today as Tasmania, but instead, the winds forced him north, leading him and his men to the southeastern coast of Australia. As fate would have it, they were the first Europeans to land in this area. Cook recorded in his journal, "THURSDAY, 19th. At 5, set the Topsails close reef'd, and 6, saw land extending from North-East to West, distance 5 or 6 Leagues, having 80 fathoms, fine sandy bottom. … The Southermost point of land we had in sight…I judged to lay in the Latitude of 38 degrees 0 minutes South and in the Longitude of 211 degrees 7 minutes West from the Meridian of Greenwich. I have named it Point Hicks, because Lieutenant Hicks was the first who discover'd this Land. To the Southward of this point we could see no land, and yet it was clear in that Quarter, and by our Longitude compared with that of Tasman's, the body of Van Diemen's land ought to have bore due South from us, and from the soon falling of the Sea after the wind abated I had reason to think it did; but as we did not see it, and finding the Coast to trend North-East and South-West, or rather more to the Westward, makes me Doubtfull whether they are one land or no. However, every one who compares this Journal with that of Tasman's will be as good a judge as I am; but it is necessary to observe that I do not take the Situation of Vandiemen's from the

Printed Charts, but from the extract of Tasman's Journal, published by Dirk Rembrantse. ... What we have as yet seen of this land appears rather low, and not very hilly, the face of the Country green and Woody, but the Sea shore is all a white Sand."

Landing of Captain Cook at Botany Bay, 1770, by E. Phillips Fox (1902)

Cook next sailed the Endeavor north, exploring the coastline and making copious notes until he came upon a wide inlet, at which point the crew anchored and Cook and some of his men actually went ashore. Cook wrote, "Sunday, 6th. In the evening the Yawl return'd from fishing, having Caught 2 Sting rays weighing near 600 pounds. The great quantity of plants Mr. Banks and Dr. Solander found in this place occasioned my giving it the Name of Botany Bay. It is situated in the Latitude of 34 degrees 0 minutes South, Longitude 208 degrees 37 minutes West. It is capacious, safe, and Commodious; it may be known by the land on the Sea Coast, which is of a pretty even and moderate height, Rather higher than it is inland, with steep rocky Clifts next the Sea, and looks like a long Island lying close under the Shore. ... We Anchor'd near the South Shore about a Mile within the Entrance for the Conveniency of Sailing with a Southerly wind and the getting of Fresh Water.... The Country is woody, low, and flat as far in as we could see, and I believe that the Soil is in general sandy. In the Wood are a variety of very beautiful birds, such as Cocatoos, Lorryquets, Parrots, etc., and crows Exactly like those we have in England. Water fowl is no less plenty about the head of the Harbour, where there is large flats of sand and

Mud, on which they seek their food; the most of these were unknown to us, one sort especially, which was black and white, and as large as a Goose, but most like a Pelican. On the sand and Mud banks are Oysters, Muscles, Cockles, etc., which I believe are the Chief support of the inhabitants, who go into Shoald Water with their little Canoes and peck them out of the sand and Mud with their hands, and sometimes roast and Eat them in the Canoe, having often a fire for that purpose, as I suppose, for I know no other it can be for."

Cook also recorded his observations about the indigenous people: "The Natives do not appear to be numerous, neither do they seem to live in large bodies, but dispers'd in small parties along by the Water side. Those I saw were about as tall as Europeans, of a very dark brown Colour, but not black, nor had they woolly, frizled hair, but black and lank like ours. No sort of Cloathing or Ornaments were ever seen by any of us upon any one of them, or in or about any of their Hutts; from which I conclude that they never wear any. Some that we saw had their faces and bodies painted with a sort of White Paint or Pigment. Altho' I have said that shell fish is their Chief support, yet they catch other sorts of fish, some of which we found roasting on the fire the first time we landed; some of these they strike with Gigs, and others they catch with hook and line; we have seen them strike fish with gigs, and hooks and lines are found in their Hutts. … However, we could know but very little of their Customs, as we never were able to form any Connections with them; they had not so much as touch'd the things we had left in their Hutts on purpose for them to take away. During our stay in this Harbour I caused the English Colours to be display'd ashore every day, and an inscription to be cut out upon one of the Trees near the Watering place, setting forth the Ship's Name, Date, etc."

A plaque commemorating Captain Cook's landing place

Cook's expedition may have been for the purposes of science on the surface, but when he claimed the new territory, the British realized it might serve as a center of future British maritime power and trade in the region.

In 1785, the French mounted a "scientific" expedition to the South Pacific with the ostensible purpose of mapping and exploration. On board were some 60 French convicts, intent, according to British espionage sources, on establishing a naval base on the shores of New Holland.

When news of this reached the imperial establishment in Britain, it was gripped by the sudden urgency to establish a British colony before the French could get there and do the same. Leading the effort to take practical possession of New Holland was eminent British gentleman scientist and naturalist Joseph Banks, president of the Royal Geographic Society and a major figure in British exploration. Banks had accompanied Cook on his preliminary voyage to New Holland, and he was generally regarded in British circles as the leading = authority on Australia. Having earlier declared the territory unfit for British colonization, he now championed colonization with a furious passion. Supported by the Society and by the extremely influential board of the British East India Company, the British establishment responded quickly. Thus, on May 13, 1787, the "First Fleet" set sail.

The fleet of 11 ships was commanded by Captain Arthur Phillip, and a race with the French was on. It was not known precisely where the French fleet was, but it was understood, or perhaps hoped, that the hastily assembled British expedition had the jump. To be safe, three of the faster ships in the fleet quickly broke away, arriving in Botany Bay on January 18, 1788.

Phillip, a man of enormous competence and extremely decided opinions, felt, after a few days, that Botany Bay did not meet the needs of a settlement, so he moved the entire fleet a few miles north up the coast to Port Jackson. The expedition dropped anchor in a sheltered harbor, and the site was named Sydney Cove, now more or less the site of the Royal Botanical Gardens. The settlement that grew up around Port Jackson took on the name Sydney, in honor of the British Home Secretary Lord Sydney.

Phillip

Greg O'Beirne's picture of a statue of Phillip on the site

Meanwhile, the French fleet arrived in Botany Bay narrowly behind the British, and as they did, Phillip dispatched a small force to Norfolk Island in order to claim that before the French could gather their senses. The French lingered for a while, but the deed was done, and New Holland, demarcated by common understanding as the eastern coast of Terra Australis, was effectively British.

At least initially, this did not change much. The British had made preliminary landfall on the Australian coast and established a nascent colony, but that hardly opened the door to immediate dominance of the South Pacific. Nonetheless, it was a major moment in the imperial machinations of the age, as history would later prove. Technically, the British were now in a position to potentially project power across the South Pacific to Spanish America, but perhaps most importantly, the British could now challenge the Spanish claim to the northwest coast of the American continent. It also positioned the British to challenge French and Dutch holdings in the Far East, and to better protect British interests in India, which by then was emerging as the virtual treasury of the British Empire.

The British cover story for all of this was the establishment of an overseas penal colony, which fooled no one. This story apart from the fact that it would in due course become a self-fulfilling prophecy, was aimed as much at opposition within the United Kingdom as to the French or the Dutch. There was a great deal of domestic opposition to the establishment of a British colony in such a remote location, and one so disconnected from Europe at that. Captain Phillip was installed as the first Governor of the Colony, the colony of New South Wales, which was formally established on January 26, 1788. Soon afterwards, Phillip wrote to his sponsor, Lord Shelburne, the ex-prime minister, that "it will be four years at least, before this Colony will be able to support itself. Still, My Lord, I think that perseverance will answer every purpose proposed by Government, and that this Country will hereafter be a most valuable acquisition to Great Britain from its situation." In both cases, Governor Phillip would prove right.

The British territorial claim on the east coast of New Holland comprised everything eastward of 135 degrees east, and all the islands of the Pacific Ocean between Cape York and the southern tip of Tasmania, then known as Van Diemen's Land. This included Norfolk Island and New Zealand.

The convict system was the reason that the colony was founded, and it was the reason thereafter why it was maintained. No developed nation on Earth had a harsher criminal code than the British at that time. Convicts were transported from England to New South Wales in hired transport ships, contracted by, among others, the British East India Company, and frequently carried in recommissioned slave ships put out of business by the abolition. The company of Camden, Calvert and King was also involved, and it was probably the largest transport contractor of the period. The partnership had originally been formed as a whaling fleet, only to subsequently transition into one that transported slaves across the Atlantic and convicts to New South Wales.

Since the entire colony was regarded as a prison, the prison blocks that were built were used only as punishment for transgressions committed in the colony. In general, the prison population was at liberty to work and live without restriction, but flogging was a standard punishment, and executions were very frequent. In the absence of a strong civil administration, local regimes could certainly be arbitrary and brutal, and of course convicts (especially women) were vulnerable to abuse at the hands of the settlers to whom they were assigned. Those deemed irredeemable even after being flogged and incarcerated were sent to the settlement of Norfolk Island, where a more formal system of incarceration was established, and where treatment of prisoners was extremely harsh.

Eventually, a settlement was founded on Norfolk Island in 1788, mainly to relieve pressure on resources in Sydney. Phillip then sent various expeditions in search of somewhere with better soils, and in due course a site was identified at what is today the Sydney suburb of Parramatta. Another was placed at Toongabbie. While difficulties continued, under the momentum of convict labor, a formal settlement soon began to take shape. Sydney Cove developed as a port, but most of the early population moved inland and settled.

Development and Expansion

"The cenotaphs of species dead elsewhere, that in your limits leap and swim and fly." – Bernard O'Dowd

The discovery of a practical route through the Blue Mountains set in motion an entire shift of attitude both inside and outside of the growing colony of New South Wales. From a thorough disinterest in immigration to the colony, other than for its essential administrative needs, the British government began suddenly promoting immigration, signaling in many ways the beginning of the end of penal transportation and the establishment of a more traditional British colony. All of this would take time since the administration of the colony was bedeviled by time and distance, but before long, it was the immigrant ship that slowly began to replace the convict ship as the most common sight in Port Jackson's harbor. The British press, now better informed, began reporting on the opportunities available in the new Australian colony, where land grants were easily obtainable and where a man of modest capital could lay claim to an acreage exceeding the wealthiest squires of England.

In 1818, the Home Secretary, 1st Viscount Sidmouth, addressed the House of Commons. In his speech, he remarked that the dread of transportation was now a thing of the past, and that it had been succeeded by a common desire for immigration to that colony that had once held such terrors. This created a situation whereby the lot of the transported convict was deemed less horrifying, and incidents were recorded of British soldiers stationed in Australia committing felonious crimes in order to secure the permanent right of abode in the new colony, and some of the benefits bestowed on emancipists once they entered free life. Emancipists were, indeed, quite often able to integrate and live entirely normal lives, availing themselves of land allocations, entering the various branches of the administration, and periodically appearing on the bench and the executive. By the end of Governor Lachlan Macquarie's term of office, in 1821, some 40,000 souls resided in Sydney and the various satellite settlements of the colony, and some 350,000 acres of land lay under occupation.

Viscount Sidmouth

In fact, the governorship of Major-General Lachlan Macquarie, between 1810 and 1821, marked something of a sea change in this regard. His predecessor, William Bligh, who was notorious for being cast adrift during the mutiny on the *Bounty*, brought his brutal and uncompromising attitude to the administration of the colony. He inherited a system of gubernatorial autocracy not dissimilar to his Navy command, and of it he made very similar use. The distance from Britain, and the nature of the colony in its early years tended to justify this. The colony was in practical terms a prison with a superficial free administration, and Bligh and his predecessors had felt obliged to rule the settlement in the manner of prison governors.

Bligh

Macquarie, however, although arriving in the colony with similar powers, was of an inclination to modernize and streamline a very primitive system of the government of New South Wales.[1] It cannot be said that he removed himself entirely from high handed and dictatorial practices of his predecessors, but he is typically regarded as the last of the tyrants, and William Bligh was certainly the worst of these.

---

[1] At that time, Van Diemen's Land was a dependency of New South Wales.

Macquarie

Macquarie arrived with a battalion of the 73rd Regiment of Foot. Part of his mandate, and certainly the reason that he arrived so heavily armed, was to bring to heel and dissolve the New South Wales Corps. The NSWC, an unruly body of armed men, were raised initially to police the colony, but they were prone to corruption, undisciplined, and certainly antagonistic towards the administration. Some decommissioned members remained in the colony, and some were absorbed into the 73rd, but most were repatriated back to England. From that point onwards, until 1870, a detachment of Imperial troops was rotated in the colony for the time being, removing the role of defense from any locally constituted militia.

Macquarie, therefore, governed with the same overarching authority as his predecessors, but under his term, the first discussion of the formation of some sort of advisory council as a precursor to the establishment of a domestic legislature was heard. The matter was put before the House of Commons in 1812, and it was agreed that such a council would be desirable, but this was promptly overruled by the Secretary of State for the Colonies, the Earl of Bathurst, who was disinclined to consider a diminishment of the powers of his office in favor of any local body. The authority of Whitehall was exercised through his appointed governor. Nonetheless, the matter was now on the table, and inevitably at some point it would be acted upon.

In the meanwhile, Macquarie's term of office witnessed quite a number of other innovations, namely a review of judicial practice and a revision of the status and role of emancipists in the colony who had by then grown considerably in number. There were inevitable social discrepancies between free settlers and emancipists, perhaps most acutely observable in the unequal distribution of land, still a procedure very much in the hands of the governor. This process had hitherto tended to favor the "exclusives," or free settlers, who numbered far less.[2] Correcting this imbalance became one of Macquarie's principal objectives. He noted, "Once a convict has become a free man, he should in all respects be considered on a footing with every other man in the colony, according to his rank in life and character." This, all things considered, was rather progressive, but it won him few very friends among the free settler community.

It is also interesting to note that Macquarie's expectation on arriving in New South Wales was to encounter a society dominated by the scrapings of His Majesty's prison system. He was, however, most surprised, and no doubt gratified, to encounter among the convicts and emancipists a great many men of education, breeding, and character, in particular among the political prisoners. Here he recognized a valuable resource, and he set about the task of better integrating these men into colonial society.

This certainly held out better prospects of success than it might have if he had tried the same thing in England. It was in the nature of the emerging Australian character to shed the rigid class conventions of England, adopting instead a more egalitarian system of social hierarchy based on meritocracy rather than aristocracy, and indeed, the airs and graces of the British upper classes were often not well tolerated in the colony.

Despite this, and despite the dearth of well-qualified men in the colony, it took a considerable amount of effort and maneuver to bring about what was a minor social revolution. Although not altogether successful, Macquarie attempted to diversify the administration, and in the end, his main achievement was probably to open the way for emancipists to serve in the judiciary, and on the bench. "I have taken upon myself to adopt a new line of conduct, conceiving that emancipation, when united with rectitude and long-tried good conduct, should lead a man back to that rank in society which he had forfeited, and do away, in as far as the case will admit, with all retrospect of former bad conduct."

These still comprised relatively small steps, especially considering that leaders back in London still did not picture the colony as anything more than a prison camp. Inevitably, however, the next phase of administrative development would be the establishment of some sort of constitutional government in the colony.

Macquarie might have been of a somewhat more democratic frame of mind than his predecessors, but he was still susceptible to arbitrary rule, rumors of which periodically washed

---

[2] "Exclusives." Defined by Encyclopedia Britannica as: *[A] member of the sociopolitical faction of free settlers, officials, and military officers of the convict colony of New South Wales.*

up on the shores of Whitehall. The story is told of a free man who was flogged on Macquarie's orders with no due process observed, and when the man appeared back in England, scarified stripes and all, his story was believed. As was customary, a commission of inquiry was authorized with a wide term of reference to examine the laws and regulations of the colony, the usages of the settlement, the system of government and the treatment of convicts, after which it was expected to make recommendations for an overhaul.

The commission began its investigation in 1819, remaining in Sydney for two years. Macquarie's maneuvers to place emancipists on the magisterial bench were not universally well-received by the commissioners, and in fact, the governor himself was not particularly complimented in the final report. His term of office, however, was in any case drawing to an end, and by 1824 he was dead.

His successor, Major General Thomas Brisbane, would enter upon his term of office under comprehensibly revised terms of service, and Brisbane would be the first governor of New South Wales whose powers were limited by statute. In 1823, upon publication of the Commission's report, the House of Commons passed the New South Wales Judicature Act, which established for the first time a legislative council.

This was not quite yet home rule, or even representative rule, but it was a start. The Legislative Council would consist of not more than seven, and no fewer than five members, and it served in practical terms only as an advisory committee for the governor, appointed by the Crown and only empowered to debate bills tabled by the governor. However, crucially, if the governor proposed a law, and a simple majority of the Legislative Council did not approve it, that law could proceed no further except on appeal to the Imperial Government.

This was certainly a significant advance in the context of government to date, meaning in practical terms that the powers of the governor were now limited and superintended. The Act of 1823, incidentally, also introduced a Supreme Court, presided over by a Chief Justice.

As time progressed, the number of councillors seated on the legislature was bumped up to a maximum of 15. Another major development at about this time was the establishment of an independent press. Prior to this, the official *Sydney Gazette* existed as a vehicle for the publication of government notices, with the occasional addition of local news.

Into this picture walked a career politician by the name of William Charles Wentworth, who arrived in New South Wales in 1824, bringing with him a printing press. Wentworth is an interesting character, and his name would resonate through Australian politics for generations to come. He was, indeed, almost the quintessential colonial boy. His father, ostensibly a convict, arrived on the shores of Australia on board the *Neptune* in 1789, landing in Sydney with a heavily pregnant wife, who soon afterwards gave birth.[3]

Wentworth

William Wentworth grew up in the Parramatta settlement, where his father acquired land and prospered. Later he returned to England for his education, but was back in New South Wales by 1810, and three years later, it was he who accompanied Gregory Blaxland and William Lawson on their pathfinding exploration of the Blue Mountains. Later still, while back in England, he studied law at Cambridge and was accepted into the bar. He authored the first book to be written in Australia, the ponderously titled *A Statistical, Historical, and Political Description of the Colony of New South Wales and Its Dependent Settlements in Van Diemen's Land, With a Particular Enumeration of the Advantages Which These Colonies Offer for Emigration and Their Superiority in Many Respects Over Those Possessed by the United States of America*.

Back in the colony, he acquired land, some independently and some inherited, and before long he rose to become one of the wealthiest men in New South Wales. He was, however, a political animal, and notwithstanding his achievements in law, agriculture, and exploration, it is for his political work in the young colony that he is best remembered.

Soon after his return to the colony from his studies overseas, the first edition of the Australian was published. The *Australian* was the first newspaper produced in the colony outside of government control. Described as a vigorously critical organ of opinion, it was not very long before the *Australian* was engaged in a furious editorial campaign against the government, arguing not least for freedom of the press, but also for representative government, the abolition of transportation, and trial by jury. He was a bitter critic of the governor, General Sir Ralph

---

[3] Wentworth's father, D'Arcy Wentworth, was not transported, but slipped out of Ireland ahead of the law after four convictions for highway robbery.

Darling, and the "exclusives" who would not grant him entry into their circle upon the suspicion, and the carefully cultivated rumor, that his father was a convict.

Darling

This feud took many forms, and although the *Australian* was undoubtedly antagonistic on many occasions, often simply for the sake of it, its publication nonetheless sowed the seeds of a vigorous free press that would permeate widely as the century progressed.

In 1827, Governor Darling attempted to implement a licensing system to monitor, tax and control what he saw as an unruly press, but when heard by the judiciary, it was not upheld, which in itself marked a significant advance. One of the great conundrums of the early establishment of the colony was indeed the system of justice and law which initially fell directly under the aegis of the governor's wide sweep of powers. Inevitable, however, that venerable English institution, trial by jury, would demand implantation in the Australian colonies. However, a unique issue in a social environment dominated by convicts or ex-convicts was the guarantee under law that a man or woman might be tried by a jury of peers, and under current social conditions, a free colonist could not reasonably regard a convict, current or past, as a peer. Initially, trial was usually by Judge-Advocate and six naval or military officers, although after the Acts of 1823 and 1828, an individual could request a jury if he or she desired.

This issue divided the two main political movements in the colony, the emancipists and the exclusives, with the former led by William Wentworth. Governor Darling for once was not at loggerheads with Wentworth, and in responding to pressure from England, a bill was introduced into the legislature and passed in 1830. It allowed for trial by jury, including jury service by emancipists so long as they had not been convicted of a serious crime.

It can be said, therefore, that early limitations placed on the authority of the governor, the freedom of the press and the implementation of trial by jury were the first three major steps in the direction of constitutional liberty. However, the legislative council remained an unelected body, appointed by the Crown through the office of the governor, and could not therefore be described as representative. Full representative government would not be implemented until the abolition of transportation, and until four new colonies had been established in Australia.

Further Exploration

"As I stood, the first intruder on the sublime solitude of these verdant plains, as yet untouched by flocks and herds, I felt conscious of being the harbinger of mighty changes there." - Thomas Mitchel, explorer

Notwithstanding the narrow parameters governing the settlement of the colony, adventurous spirits always looked beyond the first range of mountains, wondering what lay beyond. At that point almost nothing was known; the settled regions of the Port Jackson hinterland comprised an area comparable to Sicily in relation to continental Europe, and aside from the fact Mathew Flinders had confirmed that it was a continent and not an archipelago, even the outline of the coast was sparsely mapped and imperfectly understood.

The first probe into the great unknown was the Blaxland-Lawson expedition, which sought to forge a passage through the Blue Mountains, and that endeavor concluded in the discovery of the Bathurst Plain. The process then continued with the journeys of George Bass and Mathew Flinders.

Bass

Flinders

While on his circumnavigation of the continent, Flinders encountered a French survey vessel, the *Géographe*, under the command of Captain Nicholas Baudin. The *Géographe* was in Australian waters with the knowledge and permission of the British authorities, and a guarantee of its protection had been issued by the Admiralty, but nonetheless, there was inevitably suspicion in regards to its intentions. A plea by its captain that the ship's mission was purely scientific was officially accepted, but a close eye was kept on it nonetheless. When the ship returned to Europe, however, a chronicle of its voyage was published, offering up French nomenclature for geographic features already visited by British ships.[4] Spencer's Gulf, for example, lying to the west of modern Adelaide, became Golfe Bonaparte, and the adjacent St

---

[4] Readers might perhaps recall that Mathew Flinders was detained on *Ille de France* for a period of time during which the French version of the map was published. Much information was cribbed from Flinders notes, and no doubt his detention was at least in part to give the French the opportunity to publish first.

Vincent's Gulf was renamed Golfe Joséphine. The entire region from the head of the Great Australian Bight to William's Promontory, over 2,000 miles of coastline, was named Terre Napoléon.

Bearing in mind the tenor of relations between Britain and France at this time, this could hardly have been interpreted in any other way than an expression of French designs on establishing colonies on Terra Australis. There is no firm historical evidence to support any real French ambitions to do so, but Baudin's expedition galvanized the authorities both in England and in New South Wales to enter upon a more urgent program of settlement. This was in order to establish a British presence more firmly on sections of the coastline still practically open to the flag of any nation.

In 1803, under Governor Phillip King, it was decided that the region most vulnerable to French colonization was Van Diemen's Land (modern Tasmania), so it was there that official attention turned first. In September 1803, the HMS *Lady Nelson*, a Royal Navy survey ship under Lieutenant John Bowen, landed at a point called Risdon Cove on the River Derwent, now part of the urban sprawl of Hobart (the current capital of Tasmania). There a military camp was established, but it was moved a year later to Sullivan's Cove, close to the center of present-day Hobart. Hobarton, as it was then known, was named by the first Lieutenant-Governor of Van Diemen's Land, Captain David Collins, in honor of the then Secretary of State for War and the Colonies, Robert Hobart, 4th Earl of Buckinghamshire, the Lord Hobart.

Lord Hobart

In October 1803, it was Captain David Collins who disembarked nearly 300 convicts at Port Phillip, close to the site of present-day Melbourne, accompanied by a small detachment of marines and a small civil staff. One of the most interesting tales to emerge from this era of Australian settlement is that of William Buckley, a transportee from Macclesfield, Cheshire, who was convicted for having received a roll of cloth knowing it to have been stolen. Having arrived in Port Phillip aboard the HMS *Calcutta*, and largely left to their own devices on shore, Buckley and three friends slipped away and made their way around the bay. While his two companions opted in the end to return and were never seen again, Buckley continued on, eating shellfish and berries until he was befriended by Aboriginals from the Watourong tribe who appeared to believe that he was a reincarnation of their dead tribal chief. For 33 years, William Buckley lived with the Watourong, learning their language, taking an Aboriginal wife, and fathering several children. In 1836, he emerged from this life and rejoined his own society, serving as an interpreter after receiving a pardon from the Lieutenant-Governor of Van Diemen's Land, Sir George Arthur.

An 1840 depiction of the landing at Melbourne

As fate would have it, the Port Phillip settlement did not last long, and in fact remained in situ for less than a year although an informal settlement remained behind after the departure of the official expedition. This was the case with quite a number of early attempts to establish settlements, and the reason was largely because they were not necessary other than as a point to hoist the Union Jack. Port Jackson and surrounding communities could hardly desire more space to expand, and it was generally understood that the Bathurst Plain offered an almost endless amount of land and resources. Therefore, once the fear of foreign invasion eased, new settlements often withered away and were abandoned.

The next settlement to be established was Port Dalrymple, founded on the north shore of Van Diemen's Land to ensure a British presence in the Bass Strait. With a better understanding of the geography of the region, this was rightly recognized as an important sea lane and trading route in the future British development of the region. This expedition was entrusted to Lieutenant Colonel William Patterson, an officer of the New South Wales Corps who arrived at the mouth of the River Tamar in November 1804, settling first at Yorktown and then a little later at Georgetown.

In October 1805, the French fleet was decimated at the Battle of Trafalgar, shattering not only French naval ambitions, but also entirely removing any threat of a French naval expedition against any British colony anywhere. 10 years later, Napoleon would be defeated at Waterloo, and with the French subdued, India was at last removed from any threat of a French takeover. Spain was disintegrating as a great imperial power, Portugal had its hands full holding on to what it had and the Dutch had ceased to occupy a place among the great trading nations of Europe. Thus, Australia was more secure, so the urgency to establish settlements therefore abated somewhat. With that, the British could at their leisure assert their imperial claim to the totality of Australia.

In the 1820s, Australia remained almost wholly unexplored, but more strategic points were identified and occupied. The settlement of Westernport took place between 1824 and 1827. Westernport, consisting of about 50 convicts, did not last for long, but Albany, similarly settled, did survive and eventually became permanent. The Melville Island settlement also did not endure for long but was moved soon afterwards to the mainland at Raffles Bay, the site of present-day Fort Wellington, where it became the basis of the city of Darwin.

In 1829, a momentous article of legislation was passed in the British House of Commons that declared the jurisdiction of the British governor general to be the entire Australian continent. In practical terms, this meant that Britain laid formal claim to Australia in total as an imperial possession. No one else was in a position to argue, and no one did.

The seeding of settlements, therefore, continued at a more measured pace, and in that year, Captain Charles Fremantle, commanding the HMS *Challenger*, entered the Swan River and dropped anchor in one of the most superb natural harbors in the world. This, the site of the future Perth, was claimed by Fremantle as part of the wider British claim to "all that part of New Holland which is not included within the territory of New South Wales." This, in essence, meant that the western half of the continent would theoretically be a colony separate of New South Wales. New South Wales, for the time being, comprised the entire eastern half of the continent, almost all of which remained completely unexplored.

Fremantle

George Pit Morison's painting of the founding of Perth

    This would not be the end to the matter, but in the meantime, as men were dropped in lands entirely unknown and given the basic means to survive, they naturally began to probe more deeply inland to see what lay beyond the dunes and cliffs. As a result, most of the early explorers were merely settlers and homesteaders engaged in breaking the ground and establishing a widely dispersed system of smallholdings, farms and homesteads. There were certainly those, mainly later in the century, who undertook epic journeys of exploration, for their own sake and for the sake of science, but most of the map of early Australia was drawn by settlers themselves, adding to the body of knowledge in increments.

In 1815, the town of Bathurst became the first inland settlement in Australia, and a road was cut across the Blue Mountains to facilitate it. The scope of interest now shifted to what was in effect the drainage system of two vast rivers, the Murray and the Darling, collected from multiple tributaries flowing off the western slopes of the Barrier Range. These rivers, while richly watering the plains below, flowed on thereafter parts unknown, and figuring out where the waters ran triggered a series of formal explorations which very quickly began to bring the interior geography of the continent into the scope of European knowledge.

The first two significant rivers discovered and named on the far side of the Blue Mountains were both named after the governor, becoming the Lachlan and the Macquarie. Both of these were subject to preliminary exploration by the the Surveyor General of New South Wales, John Oxley. Two journeys were mounted in 1817, and in each case, Oxley followed the river by boat and foot. The season was dry, however, and the water in both cases dispersed into wetlands before disappearing altogether. Nonetheless, although rather inconclusive, this short series of journeys, mild by the standards of early 19th century exploration, ultimately revealed what Oxley described as "a country of running waters: on every hill a spring and in every valley a rivulet." This was of great importance because it revealed a landscape yielding to the plough, well watered and of such vast breadth that it would answer to the needs of agricultural expansion for generations.

Oxley

On the banks of the Brisbane River, on the east coast of New South Wales, first explored by Oxley in 1823, a colony was founded with the specific purpose of containing convicts and prisoners convicted of further crimes during their period of penal service. The river was further explored in 1825 by Major Edmund Lockyer of the 57th Regiment of Foot, who penetrated to a depth of 150 miles and returned with news of yet another fertile interior. All of this set the stage for the development of another settlement, and this later became the city of Brisbane, named in honor of then governor of New South Wales, Major General Sir Thomas Brisbane.

Lockyer

Brisbane

An 1830s depiction of Brisbane

The next significant expedition to explore the interior was led by Hamilton Hume and William Hovell, commissioned in 1824 by Governor Brisbane. The objective of this expedition was to explore the territory adjacent to the colony, and to solve the enigma of where the rivers of western New South Wales flowed. The party traveled southwest along the lee of the Barrier Range, crossing numerous rivers en route, among them the Murrumbidgee, the Murray, the Mitta-Mitta, the Owens, and the Goulburn. Eventually, they reached the western shore of Port Phillip at the site of the present-day city of Geelong. It is interesting to note that Hume and Hovell both assumed when they reached the coast that they were at Westernport, and they reported back to that effect, adding that the area held excellent prospects for settlement. It was thanks to this that Brisbane's expedition to Westernport the following year was conceived. If the settler party had entered and settled the shores of Port Phillip, the chances are it would have remained since conditions for agriculture and settlement certainly were much better.

At the same time, the mystery of the watershed and the flow of the rivers washing the western slopes of the Barrier Range remained unresolved. The next to take up this quest was Captain Charles Sturt, an officer of the 39th Regiment of Foot who in 1828 was granted approval by Governor Sir Ralph Darling to explore the Macquarie River. Hamilton Hume joined the expedition at a later date, but apart from the discovery and naming of the Darling River, as well as the confirmation that the interior of New South Wales did not comprise an interior sea, the expedition returned with relatively little to report.

Sturt

A year later, Sturt was granted a further commission to explore Murrumbidgee River, a major tributary of the Murray River. A whaleboat was portaged over the Blue Mountains and assembled on the banks of the river before an eventful journey began. In January 1829, the Murray River was reached and named.[5] Reports of hostile encounters with Aborigines suggest an unfriendly welcome in the interior, but no major episodes of violence were recorded.

---

[5] The Murray River was named after current Secretary of State for War and the Colonies, Sir George Murray.

Sturt then continued down the Murray River until its confluence with the Darling River, proving that all of the rivers flowing off the western slopes found their way to the Murray River, and by following that river to its conclusion, Sturt eventually arrived at the coast. The mouth of the Murray River, dispersed into a maze of non-navigable channels, emptied into the ocean some 30 miles south of present-day Adelaide. This was rather a disappointing conclusion because it appeared that while the Murray was navigable for a great length, it was unfortunately not accessible from the ocean.

Nonetheless, Sturt's two expeditions of 1828 and 1829 are ranked as among the most important in the history of the continent. Although there were greater adventures in exploration to follow (and Sturt's own later escapades were much more daring), the discovery of the Darling River and the exploration of the Murray mapped the principal arteries of a river system draining an area double the size of France. Perhaps more importantly, the expedition identified a vast new region ripe for permanent British settlement.

The Henty brothers, Stephen and Edward, were squatters in the standard Australian terminology. They arrived in Australia in 1832, accompanied by their father Thomas, a successful English sheep farmer from West Sussex who hoped to secure land upon which to settle. They were granted a significant landholding on the Swan River, on the west coast, by application to the Colonial Office, but after two seasons of toil, they were unable to make any practical headway. They then explored the potential of Van Diemen's Land, but they found all available arable land there already claimed.

If there was nothing for them on Van Diemen's Land, they began to consider the adjacent mainland across the Bass Strait. Numerous petitions were made to the British and colonial governments for a grant of land somewhere within the vicinity, but each time they were turned down. In the end, they decided to settle illegally.

In December 1834, the brothers landed on the shore of a wide bay between modern Melbourne and Adelaide, now known as Portland Bay, where they established a small farm and undertook whaling as an initial occupation. Nine months later, the explorer and Surveyor General of New South Wales, Thomas Mitchell, stumbled upon the Henty settlement while concluding a survey of the Darling River and was amazed by what he saw. Anchored in the bay was the privately-owned ship, the *Elizabeth*, part whaler and part supply ship, and a homestead and gardens. Everything was flourishing, with sheep that had been brought across from Van Diemen's Land. This incidentally started an industry in the future colony of Victoria that would grow considerably in the future.

The Henty brothers certainly took the initiative, although their founding of a settlement and occupation of a new quarter did not win them many friends in government. The governor of New South Wales, Major Sir George Gipps, wrote in an 1840 dispatch to the Secretary of State for the Colonies, Lord Russell, that notwithstanding the claim of the Henty brothers and others who had since followed suit that they had rendered a service to the Crown by founding the settlement at their own expense, they had in fact done no such thing. The governor then proceeded to grumble fitfully at the expenses required for furnishing the settlement with the accoutrements of civilization (like a police force) and the costs of laying out a town.

Despite official grumbling, the Henty brothers consolidated their settlement, and others joined them. In 1851, the colony of Victoria was formally established, and in 1855, Edward Henty was elected to the legislative assembly. In time, the brothers were credited with establishing the first settlement of Victoria, and they are also considered the founders of the wool industry in that colony.

There were many other unauthorized settlements and family homesteads popping up in numerous locations, some more successful than others, and while this did not account for a majority of fresh settlements, they certainly contributed a great deal to the steady dispersal of the European population.

The End of the Dream

"No English words are good enough to give a sense of the links between an Aboriginal group and its homelands." - Professor W. E. H. Stanner, *White Man Got No Dreaming*

There has tended to be a persistent myth that the Aboriginal people of Australia passively watched as Europeans entered and took over their land. This might have been true on occasions, but almost from the commencement of white settlement, hostilities and difficulties characterized the early clash of cultures.

In 1837, the Aborigine Protection Society was formed in England by a small group of British liberals with an interest in ensuring the protection of the sovereign legal and religious rights of native peoples falling under the Pax Britannia. This was a mere four years after the abolition of slavery in the British Empire, and this Society is often regarded as one of the earliest human rights organizations. Many of those active in the Society were also active in the abolition movement of a generation earlier, and this marked something of a sea change in European attitudes when it came to race and the responsibility of the empire.

In 1836, as the Henty brothers and Thomas Mitchell met on the shores of Portland Bay, a British Parliamentary select committee was assembled to investigate the conditions of aboriginal peoples in the colonies. The preamble to the report of the committee speaks somewhat to its mandate: "[To] consider what measures ought to be adopted with regards to the native inhabitants of the countries where British settlements are made, and to the neighboring tribes, in order to secure to them the due observance of justice, and the protection of their rights; to promote the spread of civilization among them, and to lead them to the peaceful and voluntary reception of the Christian religion."

This spoke to all the major settled colonies of the empire, comprising India, British North America (Canada), New Zealand, South Africa, and Australia. In every case an indigenous population lay in the path of European interests, and again, in almost every case, the results were detrimental to native societies. Some suffered more acutely than others. Indians and Africans did not succumb quite so easily to pernicious disease as the natives of North America and Australia did, and as such, once released from slavery, their numbers and general prosperity improved. However, they were still subject to rapacious European economic piracy, mostly in the seizure of their land, but also, in such colonies as Natal, in the unequal social restrictions that locked them out of normal economic development.

The formation of this select committee marked an important moment in British history, a moment in which the British Empire began to establish its essential charter. In view of British global dominance, that charter necessarily included the first official acknowledgement of a responsibility inherited by the British people to balance their global ambitions with the humane usage of the aboriginal peoples falling under British sovereignty.

In many respects, this was the essential enigma of the British Empire. In the post-slavery era, an enormous weight of conscience seemed to settle on the shoulders of the metropolitan population. In a generally liberal age, the British intelligentsia responded by seeking to ameliorate some of the worst impacts of cultural exploitation, especially once the grotesquely deleterious effects of European intrusion into new lands was understood. However, that sentiment, while powerfully expressed and felt in England, did not easily translate along the frontiers, where the practical work of founding an empire was taking place. The noble savage seemed often less noble in close proximity, and the ostensibly primitive lifestyles of those like the Australian Aborigines allowed them to be construed as something less than human, and therefore outside the social charter.

In due course, the colonial authorities in Australia would apply numerous policies of social engineering that affected the indigenous people of the federation. In the early years, however, no such finesse existed, and where the two cultures met, and where the Aborigines resisted, they were dealt with both arbitrarily and violently. For example, in Van Diemen's Land, under the governorship of Sir George Arthur, the extermination of Aborigines was pursued with vigor, even though the population was always small. Any elements that survived the onslaught of disease were mopped up later under an informal system of bounty.

Again, at odds with the popular view of Australia's Aboriginal people as a passive, spiritual and yielding race is the fact that warfare did indeed exist in their society. Although hardly on the scale of the Maori warfare in New Zealand, or the martial traditions of many South Sea Island societies, Aboriginal warfare took the form of violent skirmishes in pursuit of vendettas, women, natural resources, or local predominance. Aboriginal weapons technology was adequate for the needs of a hunter/gatherer society, but hardly the offensive equipment typically to be found in the hands of the Maoris.

It is also true that indigenous Australians, to a greater or lesser extent, lacked the scope of social organization necessary to mount anything resembling a conventional war. The experience of outward moving Australian pioneers and settlers could hardly compare, for example, to those of the South African Boer who were matched against the Zulu and the amaNdebele, two of the most effective and organized military societies in the non-European world. The Zulu, however, held a clear sense of land title (albeit communal), and they understood the concept and ramifications of white occupation. Concepts of Aboriginal land and land ownership, on the other hand, were vague and steeped in tradition. Although immensely valuable to them as a whole, conquering, occupying and defending territory simply did not exist as a concept. Likewise, the gathering of a confederation to fight a common enemy on a substantial level was also simply absent from the common mindset. The Aborigines of Australia, therefore, could hardly have been less equipped to deal with the arrival of outsiders.

Initially, however, the melee and ambush tactics of the Aborigines worked well. They easily matched the colonists' ability to defend themselves with the simple, muzzle loading black powder guns of the age. Things changed radically, however, at the moment that breech-loading and repeating rifles appeared on the scene. Mounted infantry and ad hoc settler militias began to deal ruthlessly and efficiently with the paper-thin defenses of vulnerable Aboriginal communities. Thus, the balance of power began to shift very quickly, and very much against the Aborigines.

What was known as the "Australian Frontier Wars" was little more than an ongoing attrition between the two sides that began almost immediately and continued well into the 20th century, with the last recorded fights being logged as late as the 1930s. Periodically the "war" flared into identifiable battles, but in comparison to the wars being fought in Africa and Asia, nothing that occurred during the "Black Wars" rises to anything that might be considered a major conflict. In most cases, they were simply massacres that ended up being recorded.

The first white settlements were along the banks of the Hawkesbury River, leading inland from the river mouth located a few miles up the coast from Sydney. The region was heavily populated by Aboriginal people belonging to the Darug group, a coastal foraging people whose language encompassed an area of about 2,300 square miles around Port Jackson and Botany Bay. What followed is now known as the "Hawkesbury and Nepean Wars," which, from about 1795-1816, comprised Aboriginal raids on farms and the reprisals that these provoked. In 1816, Governor Macquarie deployed a detachment of the 46th Regiment of Foot to patrol the populated reaches of the Hawkesbury River, ending in a raid on an encampment that claimed the lives of 14 Aboriginals.

Similar attacks and raids in and around Parramatta were dealt with by an official sanction, made by Governor Philip King, that Aboriginals could be legally shot on sight. This was not quite the bounty offered in Van Diemen's Land, but it placed the Aboriginals outside the protection of law, violating the essential element of the British imperial charter. Apart from the occasional rumblings of concern from afar, no real effort was made by the British government to intervene. Typically, news of an event of significance did not reach Whitehall until a year later, and another year would pass before the official reprimand was read in Sydney, at which point no one really cared anymore. In a place where convicts were being routinely flogged to within an inch of their lives, the plight of some faceless band of Aboriginals being removed from the land hardly stirred national outrage.

The various coastal settlements encountered indigenous people in almost every instance, and in some cases the contact was friendly. One example can be found in the explorations of John Oxley, who anchored at Moreton Bay in 1823 on his way back from a visit to Port Curtis, both on the east coast of modern Queensland. There he found a shipwreck survivor who had lived among the Aborigines for years in a state of harmony. Likewise, there is the tale of William Buckley, who prospered for over 30 years among the Aborigines.

In fact, examples like those might have been the rule rather than the exception had the rapacious seizure of land for private use not characterized every step taken by the British as they moved deeper into the territory. Nowhere was this more pronounced than in Tasmania. Founded as a settlement in 1803, the temperate climate and fertility of the island saw it develop a vibrant settler culture alongside the establishment of a formal penal colony. Until the abolition of penal transportation in 1868, Van Diemen's Land, alongside Norfolk Island, served as the main penal complex, and it had become extremely sophisticated by the time the penal system was dissolved. At the same time, free settlers also trickled into Van Diemen's Land in steadily growing numbers, to the extent that when the Henty Brothers arrived in the mid-1830s, no spare arable land was available. In an environment such as this, the Aborigines simply had to go, and it was Governor George Arthur who pursued an extermination policy with the greatest vigor. This followed almost 25 years of attrition as indigenous people, numbering no more than a few thousand to begin with, mounted ever more determined resistance as white settlers increasingly laid claim to the land. This was a phase also known as the "Black War," and in its local context, it has often been cited as the most effective Aboriginal resistance of the era. White fatalities numbered some 50 individuals between 1828 and 1830, compelling many rural homesteads to be fortified. A shoot on sight policy was pursued under gubernatorial decree, and a heavy-handed application of capital punishment saw the gallows serve as a major weapon of war.

Matters came to a head in 1830 when Governor Arthur sought to bring about an end to the ongoing insecurity by implementing a massive sweep across the island, known as the "Black Line." Every able-bodied male in the colony joined, including convicts, and as dwindling bands of Aborigines were flushed out and killed, resistance effectively collapsed. A broken and diminished society of indigenous Tasmanians was gathered together and exiled on Flinders Island, located to the northeast of Van Diemen's Land, where a reservation was founded under a degree of government administration.

A similar state of affairs took place on the Bathurst Plain as soon as white settlers began crossing the Blue Mountains and parceling up land for the establishment of farms. This was land occupied by the Wiradjuri people, more numerous and more aggressive in general than the Darug. Aggressive Aboriginal attacks were regularly launched against isolated homesteads, often accompanied by larceny, and these were almost always followed up by a bloody reprisal attack. Frontier law prevailed, and frontier justice was liberally applied.

In 1824, Governor Brisbane placed the settled region surrounding Bathurst under martial law, for reasons, he said, "[to end] the Slaughter of Black Women and Children, and unoffending White Men." It might also be interesting to note that it was Brisbane who established the New South Wales Mounted Police as a paramilitary protection force and an agent of law enforcement.[6] The force was initially deployed against bushrangers, another source of insecurity on the frontier, and an inevitable byproduct of such a remote penal settlement.[7]

This, then, was the state of things as the colony and its various settlements slowly took root across Australia, and the dispersed aboriginal community had to digest the bitter threat that this represented to their society and way of life. As further colonies were added to the evolving commonwealth, the violent dispossession of indigenous people accelerated. Matters would not be taken up by a native affairs administration in any meaningful way until the early 1960s, and prior to that, moral responsibility for Aboriginal protection and well-being lay largely with Christian missionaries.

The Founding of Western Australia

"Still round the corner there may wait a new road or a second secret gate>" - J.R.R. Tolkien

The next major advance in the development of the Australian colonies was the establishment of Western Australia. The first formal settlement was Albany, and at more or less the same time these colonists were finding their feet on the shores of King George's Sound, the first formal survey of the Swan River was taking place under the command of Captain James Stirling aboard the HMS *Success*. This survey was undertaken in the usual Royal Navy style, accompanied by various technical experts and summarized in a succinct report that contained a great deal of positive commentary on the potential of the surrounding country for settlement. As soon as that report found its way onto the desk of Governor Darling, plans were made to establish a permanent settlement.

---

[6] The New South Wales Mounted Police remains part of the New South Wales Police Force. It was founded on 7 September 1825, recruited from a British military regiment stationed in NSW at the time. Its mandate was to protect travellers, suppress convict escapees and fight indigenous Australians.

[7] *Bushrangers* were in the main escaped convicts adopting a life as outlaws and relying on robbery for survival. The most famous of these was Ned Kelly.

The usual fears of the French pitching their tent in a British sphere of interest were augmented somewhat on this occasion by a fear that the Americans might do the same thing. The mouth of the Swan River offered the only safe anchorage on the west coast of Australia, and if Britain did not actively claim it, there was every reason to suppose that someone else would. It is also worth bearing in mind that the almost infinite scope for growth and development in New South Wales discouraged rigorous exploration elsewhere, so as far as the British government was concerned, dumping a handful of convicts on the site and hoisting the Union Jack would, for the time being at least, be enough to stake a legal British claim.

There was, however, a momentum gathering of private capital engaging in proxy imperial endeavors, as evidenced by the enormous influence of the Hudson Bay Company and the British East India Company. Both controlled vast regions with virtual monopolies on every available resource and very little in the way of direct imperial control. By then, the Australian Agricultural Company, with a starting capital of £1,000,000, was active in New South Wales, and the Van Diemen's Land Company operated in that colony. Private capital, therefore, found itself extremely interested in the prospects of Western Australia.

One of the first Britons to show such interest was Thomas Peel, the cousin of future Prime Minister Sir Robert Peel. Peel offered the government a scheme to settle 10,000 colonists at £30 per head in exchange for a grant of 4,000,000 acres of land. In response, the government scoffed, and Peel was ushered out the door, but he remained undeterred. Instead, he decided to proceed with his own resources, and upon an investment of £50,000, a colossal sum in those days, he set sail for Western Australia abroad the *Parmelia*, arriving on June 1, 1829 with 50 colonists. The *Parmelia*, incidentally, was captained by James Stirling, and it was he who chanced upon the optimum site for the establishment of a town. Perth, he later wrote, "[is] as beautiful as anything of this kind I had ever witnessed." They subsequently founded the Swan River Colony.

As the first colonists fought to establish a beachhead, more were persuaded by Peel's agents, and by January 1830, 25 ships had landed some 850 free settlers. A population of 1,300 was allotted 525,000 acres of land, and during 1830, a further 1,000 men, women, and children were landed. In short order, the basics of a vibrant British colony were established.

The early colonists in Western Australia suffered through bitter and hard experiences. In 1830, for example, there were 4,000 individuals registered as residents in the colony, but two years later that figure had dropped to only 1,300. Peel lost almost everything, and the early settlement was described as "the scarecrow of civilization." However, even as many broken people headed back to England, others remained, and despite the hardships, the Swan River Settlement survived.

The residents had no idea there were great deposits of gold buried in Australian soil there, so the settlement remained agricultural in nature. It soon became apparent, however, that this was not the type of country that could support peasant farmers of minor holdings. If anything, this area required large-scale landowners to implement stock rearing on a significant scale, and this would eventually take place. By 1840, the population had recovered, numbering above 5,000.

There was initially a determination to keep convicts out of this settlement, but labor was scarce, and as adaption to large tracts of land continued, labor in increasing quantities was required. Under the governorship of Charles Fitzgerald, a tentative program of convict importation began, formalized by an order in council of the British Parliament ratified on May 12, 1849. This resulted in the importation of some 10,000 convicts, and Perth as a consequence became a penal colony. However, a balancing number of subsidized free settlers were steadily introduced by the British government, largely as an appeasement measure against deep disquiet at the introduction of so many convicts. The advantage lay now in the availability of labor for the construction of roads and general infrastructure, and the ability to develop the plantation economy of the settlement. It was not long before Perth took root.

Once their sentences were served, many of these men drifted away to other colonies and other regions of the world, leading Fitzgerald to remark that "Western Australia is, in fact, a mere conduit pipe through which the moral sewage of Great Britain is poured upon those communities." However, thanks to the establishment and endurance of the Swan River Colony, Western Australia did indeed now lie firmly within the British sphere of influence. The experiment in subsidized immigration, organized and systematic, had worked, and this prompted further interest in systematic colonization. As a result, those in authority, both in Britain and in the growing Australian colonies, began to consider expanding the program to include the remaining unsettled regions of the vast land on the continent.

South Australia and Tasmania

"In announcing to the Colonists of His Majesty's Province of South Australia the establishment of the Government, I hereby call upon them to conduct themselves at all times with order and quietness, duly to respect the laws, and by a course of industry and sobriety, by the practice of sound morality, and a strict observance of the ordinances of religion, to prove themselves to be worthy to be the Founders of a great and free Colony." - Captain Sir John Hindmarsh, the first governor of South Australia

One of the ramifications of the Industrial Revolution was the rise of a class of urban poor. Low wages, scarce employment, the decline of cottage industries, and the growth of urban slums were symptoms of this new era, and it led to England being overpopulated at a time that the British Empire controlled vast and empty regions all around the world. Emigration was seen as an obvious solution, but Thomas Peel had suffered a financial disaster with his Swan River experiment, and there were few willing to try that method again.

However, in 1829, an alternative concept of colonization was suggested in a book entitled *A Letter from Sydney*. This book was written by Edward Gibbon Wakefield, an otherwise unremarkable man who had never left the shores of England but nevertheless presented a unique idea. Peel had premised his scheme on an abundance of cheap land, but Wakefield advocated something entirely different, suggesting that the authorities sell land in the colonies at a balanced market price. His rationale was simply that for a colony to be successful, land, capital, and labor were all required. Cheap land would attract the yeomanry to homesteading, denying the large landowner with solid capital the labor that he needed. Capital investment would not be attracted to a colony without labor, and there were colonies in what would nowadays be the developing world that offered enormous pools of indigenous labor. Obviously, a plantation economy had a better chance of getting off the ground in any one of them.

Thus, Wakefield suggested the establishment of a fund to induce white labor from England to venture to the colonies. Payment for labor would be calculated to ensure that after two or three years of work, a person who headed overseas would have saved enough to buy his own land. This would also serve to filter out the adventurers who very frequently took up land and abandoned it soon afterwards. The sale of land would fund the costs of immigration.

Wakefield formed a colonization society, and it was incorporated at almost the very same time Charles Sturt submitted his survey of the Murray River catchment to the office of the governor. In it he revealed the existence of a vast reserve of arable land, and this convenient coincidence of circumstances led to the formation of the colony of South Australia.

In 1831, the South Australia Land Company was formed, but Wakefield found the British government curiously coy about authorizing the transfer of sovereignty to a private company, even though it had few qualms about doing that elsewhere. An association was formed instead, the South Australian Association, which perhaps felt less nakedly commercial than a company, and under the condition that the new colony be ruled directly from Whitehall through a governor, a new colony was authorized. However, while the British government might technically rule, the sale of land would be supervised by a board of commissioners comprising the principal investors in the scheme, so a private facility actually pulled the strings. This would emerge in due course as the South Australia Company, founded on a capital subscription of £200,000. In the end, the British government did it on the cheap, as it so often did, by allowing private capital to pioneer the settlement and pay the bills, while at the same time claiming sovereignty over any new territory founded.

The governor appointed by the Colonial Office to rule South Australia was Royal Navy Captain Sir John Hindmarsh. The initial corps of settlers would be dropped on Kangaroo Island, lying a few miles offshore of Cape Jarvis, close to modern day Adelaide. The settlement was soon moved on to the mainland, however, and the site of Adelaide was selected as the future capital.

Hindmarsh

An 1839 depiction of Adelaide

Van Diemen's Land had continued to exist as a dependency of New South Wales, serving the function of a penal colony, but in 1825, via an act passed by Parliament, the two territories were separated and the institutions of a separate colonial government were established. As a penal colony, and under the governorship of Sir George Arthur, a man thoroughly like Bligh when it came to autocratic tendencies, Van Diemen's Land became the home of desperate men and hard cases, and the regime was suitably harsh and uncompromising. Arthur also happened to be the man who put a final end to Aboriginal resistance, which, combined with the terms of penal service on the island, stamped him and his colony with a notorious reputation.

Thanks to all of these activities, by the late 1830s, Australia consisted of the colonies of New South Wales, Van Diemen's Land (the only colony with defined borders), Western Australia, and Southern Australia. Victoria, Queensland, and the Northern Territories remained to be established. Victoria would be the next piece of the puzzle put in place, but this would not come until one of the most pivotal events of early Australian history: the discovery of gold.

The End of the Convict Era

"Twenty-five lashes under my surveillance had the same effect as 1,000 lashes under any other person's hand." – Mr. E.A. Slad, from the report of the Select Committee

If one was to draw a clean line under any episode of early Australian history, it would be the abolition of penal transportation to the continent, a practice that had defined the empire's first colonial adventures in Australia.

The beginning of the end of organized penal transportation came with the review of a parliamentary select committee undertaken between 1837 and 1838. Under the weight of two substantial reports, the essential conclusion was that transportation did not deter crime, but it did debase the social quality of the colonies. This subsequently led to a commission of inquiry, the Molesworth Commission.

Much of the impetus for both of these was the work of an early penal reformer and human rights advocate by the name of Alexander Maconochie. Maconochie was a tall and rather austere man, a Royal Navy captain and a founding member of the Royal Society who accepted the position of private secretary to Governor Sir John Franklin. Maconochie was, in effect, a spy, implanted by the liberal humanitarian movement in Britain to report back in a balanced manner on conditions for convicts on the island.

His report, when finally complete, created an enormous stir both in England and in Van Diemen's Land, the former because of the deplorable conditions described and the latter because an unwelcome light was suddenly shining on practices long kept hidden. The episode contributed to the recall of Governor John Franklin and triggered a general parliamentary review. It is also fair to note that a general movement towards liberal humanitarianism was going on back home, so the antiquated British penal code was ripe for review and revision. The great prison reformer Elizabeth Fry led a movement of interested parties, within which Maconochie was the undisputed technical expert, and this movement acknowledged the anachronistic nature of the entire tradition of transportation.

Fry

The parliamentary select committee took a great deal of testimony from influential sources within the colony, where a strong movement also existed for the practice to end. In this case it had less to do with humanitarian concerns and more to do with the unfair competition created by free labor. Of course, colonists in Australia also worried about typical security concerns that arise in a society so dominated by criminal elements.

In short, penal transportation had run its course, and it was now simply a matter of dismantling it as quickly as British parliamentary procedures would allow. Maconochie's condemnatory report prompted an immediate revision of prison conditions in lieu of abolition; up to 1836, the system had introduced a round figure of 100,000 convicts to Australia, and on that date some 45,000 remained detained under various terms in several locations. Most of these were common criminals, along with occasional political prisoners and a handful of what were quaintly known as "gentlemen convicts."

Transportation to New South Wales ended in 1840, but facilities on Norfolk Island and Van Diemen's Land remained operational, with administrative responsibility for the former shifting eventually to Hobart. Van Diemen's Land remained the only functioning penal colony, including

Norfolk Island, which was reserved as a receptacle for the hardest cases and those convicted of additional crimes during their terms of transportation.

The ongoing transportation of convicts to Van Diemen's Land was opposed by a number of local societies and organizations, including the Australasian Anti-Transportation League, various civic and church groups, and numerous organizations and bodies in the United Kingdom itself. The practice was suspended briefly in 1846, but it was quickly revived when immediate overcrowding in British metropolitan prisons began to be felt. By then, terms of imprisonment had in any case been redefined, and convicts were now termed "exiles." Since the entire system was now under consistent review, the worst excesses of treatment and conditions had eased considerably.

The last convict ship dispatched from England to Van Diemen's Land, the *St Vincent*, arrived in 1853, and the final ship to leave England, the *Hougoumont*, left in 1867 and arrived in Western Australia on January 10, 1868. Among the early colonies, South Australia was the only one that never accepted convicts from Britain, but it did accept convicts from within the region.

In tandem with the end of the convict system, British settlement became more absolute. The practical acquisition and distribution of land had always been haphazard, ad hoc, and largely unregulated, and it took a considerable amount of time for the British government to embrace the inevitability that, having set the process in motion, sovereignty over the entire continent would simply be a matter of time. The government, therefore, seemed always to be several steps behind the facts on the ground. This also was aided by the vast distances involved, the autocratic powers granted early governors, and the different styles of government that each operated. Land was handled by various governors entirely according to their own whims and inclinations, and this tendency continued until 1831, when better control of the process was assumed by Whitehall, which decreed thereafter that land could only be settled by auction.

Passage through the Blue Mountains and the land rush that followed attracted large capital. The Australian Agricultural Company, incorporated by Royal Charter, was formalized by a parliamentary act in 1824. Part of the mandate of the company was "for the cultivation and improvement of waste lands in the colony of New South Wales." A tract of land measuring 500,000 acres was made available for no payment. In the same way, the Van Diemen's Land Company, also incorporated under a Royal Charter, received 400,000 acres for an annual rental of £468.

This can be regarded as a legitimate allocation of land, at least according to the rules and regulations devised by the government. At the other end of the spectrum resided the likes of the Henty brothers and the "squatters." The term squatter, as it was applied to land occupation in Australia, was derived from a similar term employed in America that described individuals or groups occupying land without legal title. In the early days, this simply came about when a convict, having served out his term, identified a piece of unused ground, built a shanty, and began husbandry and cultivation. Usually this was accompanied by bootlegging, bushranging, and other crimes, all of which gave squatters a poor reputation.

The proliferation of squatting, especially once the land beyond the Blue Mountains had been opened up, came about entirely because there were few if any recognized regulations. It was always pointless to try and stop people from expanding outwards, and in the absence of any means of laying legal claim to title, squatting was inevitable. It is also true that land was a limitless resource at that time, so there seemed to be no point in wasting administrative resources dealing with squatting when so much land was available for anyone who wanted it. All the while, the large landowners produced crops in quantity and the accumulation of squatter production began to contribute plenty to the tax base and the growing economy. Eventually, authoritizes regulated squatter land by issuing grazing licenses and other permits for a nominal annual stipend.

By 1835, the colonial administration branches began to consider the legality of land grants issued during the era of tyrannical governors, and this briefly shook the economic foundations of the various settlements. When consulted, the law officers gave it as their opinion that every arbitrary grant of land from the date of the foundation of New South Wales were invalid. The following year, however, an act of parliament quickly regularized all of these, "…to remove such doubts and to quiet the titles of His Majesty's subjects holding or entitled to hold any land in New South Wales."

Under Governor George Gipps (1837-1846), a regulation was put into effect that allowed, by special survey, anyone depositing £5,120 to acquire thousands of acres of land wherever they chose. Before the folly of this was realized, eight such claims had been made and formalized, all in the vicinity of towns. This was a speculative venture on the part of several wealthy men, and they reaped astronomical profits within a few years, especially when urban land prices leapt in value in the aftermath of the gold rush.

Gipps

In the end, the use of the term "squatter" evolved from small-scale brigand homesteaders to imply large-scale landowners or lessees who ran significant herds of sheep. As the administration of the colonies settled into a period of constitutional government and rule of law, the regulations governing land acquisition and alienation were formalized, and attention then shifted to the evolution of the agricultural industry. Wheat and other cereals were commonly grown, but wool and sheep production emerged in New South Wales and elsewhere as the most important industry.

By the dawn of the second half of the 19th century, the constituent colonies of Australia were beginning to take on the character of satellite communities of Britain, with all of the accoutrements of a modern constitutional government. The next natural step in this process would be the quest for Responsible Government, or the devolution of substantive powers of administration away from Whitehall and to the various local colonial capitals. This would mark the beginning of modern Australian history, and it was a process that was already underway in all of Britain's overseas dominions, or at least those that enjoyed majority British populations.

By then, Australia was one of the key destinations of British emigration. By 1850, the immigrant and settler population of Australia was 400,000, and a decade later that figure would reach 1 million.

Online Resources

Other British history titles by Charles River Editors

Other titles about Australia on Amazon

Bibliography

Bach, John (1976). A Maritime History of Australia. Melbourne: Nelson. ISBN 0-17005087-4.

Barker, Anthony. What Happened When: A Chronology of Australia from 1788. Allen & Unwin. 2000. online edition

Bambrick, Susan ed. The Cambridge Encyclopedia of Australia (1994)

Basset, Jan The Oxford Illustrated Dictionary of Australian History (1998)

Broeze, Frank (1998). Island Nation: A History of Australians and the Sea. Sydney: Allen & Unwin. ISBN 9781864484243.

Davison, Graeme, John Hirst, and Stuart Macintyre, eds. The Oxford Companion to Australian History (2001) online at many academic libraries; also excerpt and text search

Galligan, Brian, and Winsome Roberts, eds. Oxford Companion to Australian Politics (2007); online at many academic libraries

Lewis, Wendy, Simon Balderstone and John Bowan (2006). Events That Shaped Australia. New Holland. ISBN 978-1-74110-492-9.

O'Shane, Pat et al. Australia: The Complete Encyclopedia (2001)

Serle. Percival, ed. Dictionary of Australian Biography (1949)online edition

Shaw, John, ed. Collins Australian Encyclopedia (1984)

Taylor, Peter. The Atlas of Australian History (1991)

Connor, John (2002). The Australian frontier wars, 1788–1838. Sydney: UNSW Press. ISBN 0-86840-756-9

Free Books by Charles River Editors

We have brand new titles available for free most days of the week. To see which of our titles are currently free, click on this link.

Discounted Books by Charles River Editors

We have titles at a discount price of just 99 cents everyday. To see which of our titles are currently 99 cents, click on this link.

CPSIA information can be obtained
at www.ICGtesting.com
Printed in the USA
LVHW052159141220
674149LV00040B/2227